#SCRUBTEC

A SNARKY ADULT COLORING BOOK FOR SURGICAL TECHNOLOGISTS

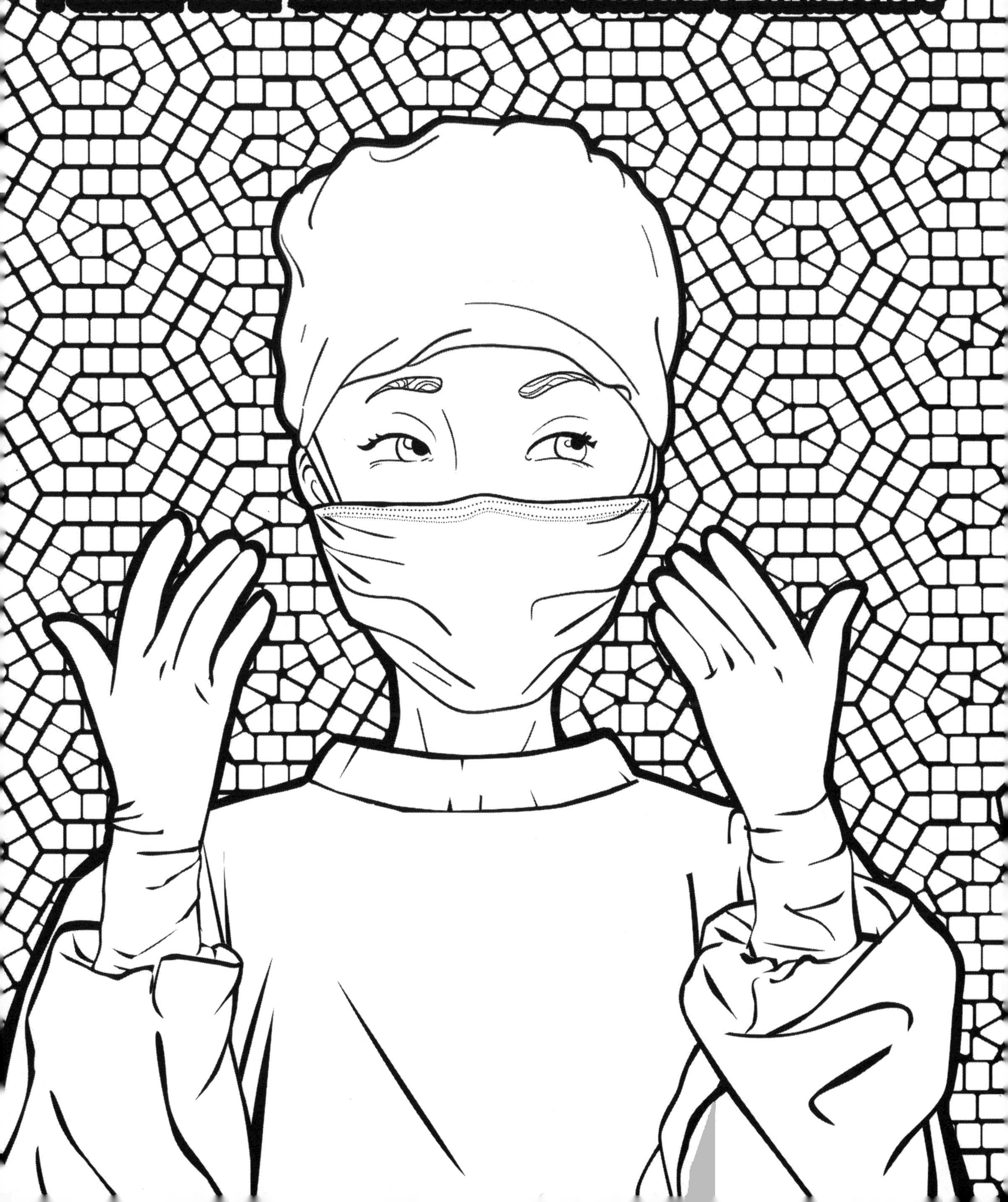

Want free goodies?
Email us at freebies@pbleu.com

@papeteriebleu

Papeterie Bleu

Shop our other books at
www.pbleu.com

Wholesale distribution through Ingram Content Group
www.ingramcontent.com/publishers/distribution/wholesale

For questions and customer service, email us at
support@pbleu.com

FREE PDF DOWNLOAD OF THIS BOOK

www.pbleu.com/scrubtech

YOUR DOWNLOAD CODE: SCRUB373

@papeteriebleu

Papeterie Bleu

I SPENT 15 MINUTES SCRUBBING IN
NOW MY BUTTHOLE ITCHES

KEEP
CALM
and
STAY
STERILE

ONLY A
Scrub
Tech
CAN UNDERSTAND
THE STRESS OF HAVING
FOUR PAIRS OF
Scissors
AND
NONE OF THEM CUT
THE WAY THE
Surgeon
WANTS.

WHEN YOU
ARE
sterile
AT A
CODE BROWN

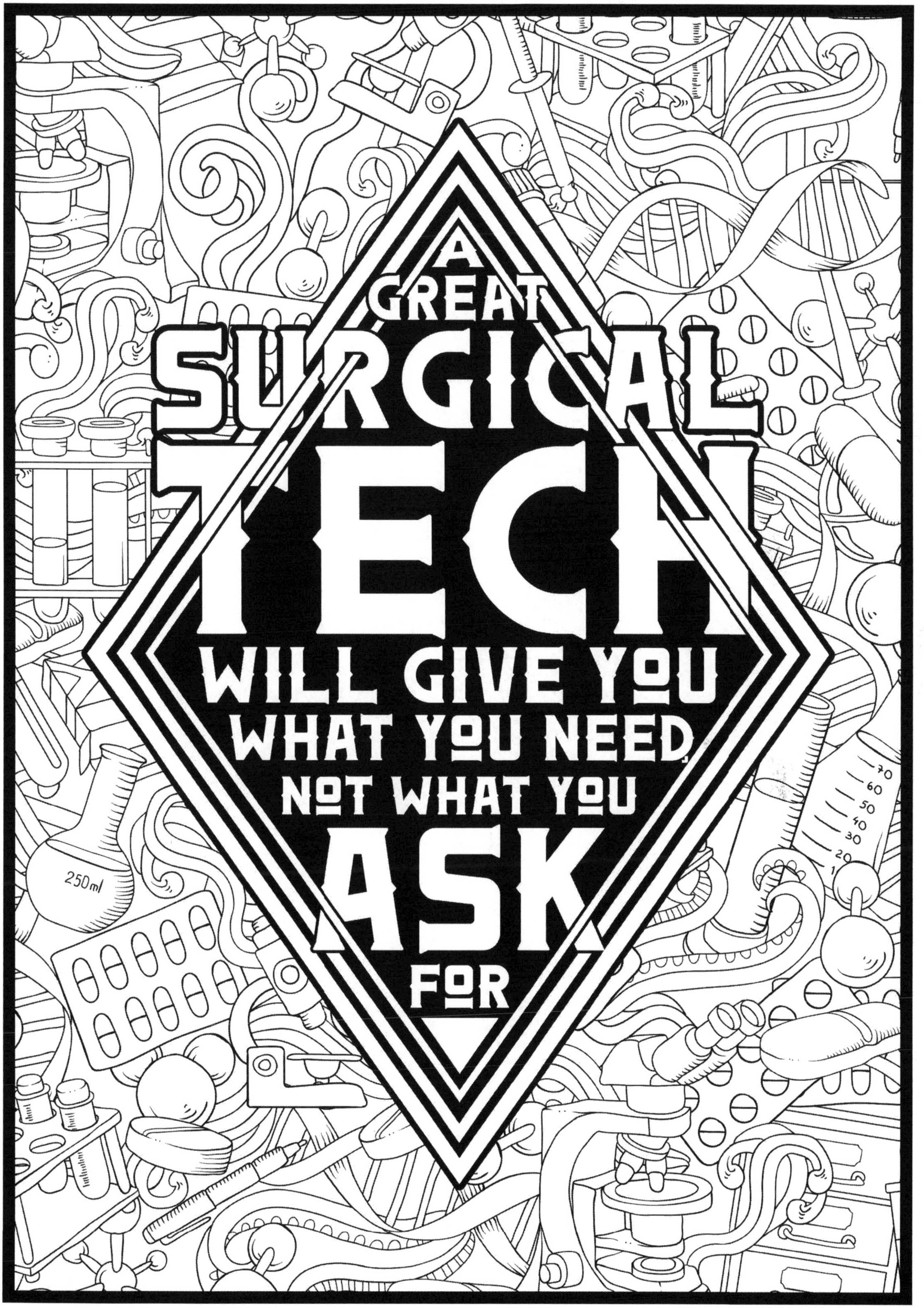
A GREAT
SURGICAL
TECH
WILL GIVE YOU
WHAT YOU NEED,
NOT WHAT YOU
ASK
FOR
250ml
70
60
50
40
30
20

YOU MIGHT BE A
Scrub Tech
IF YOU WASH YOUR HANDS
BEFORE
GOING TO THE BATHROOM

HELLO I'M
Rich
HELLO I'M
Kelly
HELLO I'M
Allis
MEET MY FRIENDS
from work

YOU MIGHT BE A
SCRUB
TECH
IF YOU'VE EVER PASSED
AN INSTRUMENT
A LITTLE HARDER
AS A FORM OF
NONVERBAL
COMMUNICATION

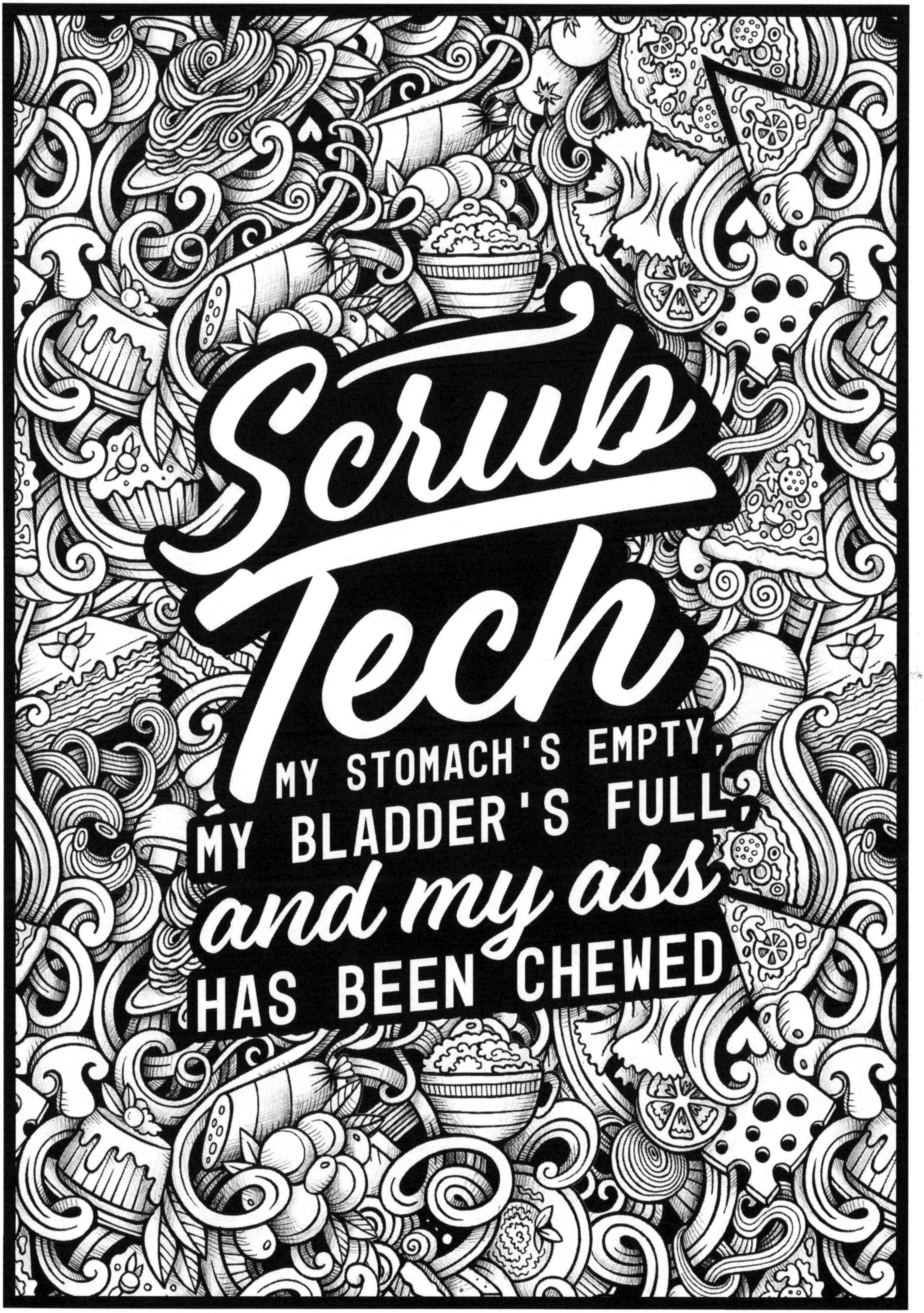
Scrub
Tech
MY STOMACH'S EMPTY,
MY BLADDER'S FULL,
and my ass
HAS BEEN CHEWED

WHEN YOUR FAVORITE SURGEON CANCELS YOUR FAVORITE SURGERY AND NOW YOU'RE STUCK DOING AN 8 HOUR EX LAP

TRAUMA
Queen
HOSPITAL
HOSPITAL

I don't curse like a
SAILOR
I curse like a
SCRUB TECH

You might be a
SURGICAL TECH
if you've ever
basted your
TURKEY
with a
TOOMEY
SYRINGE

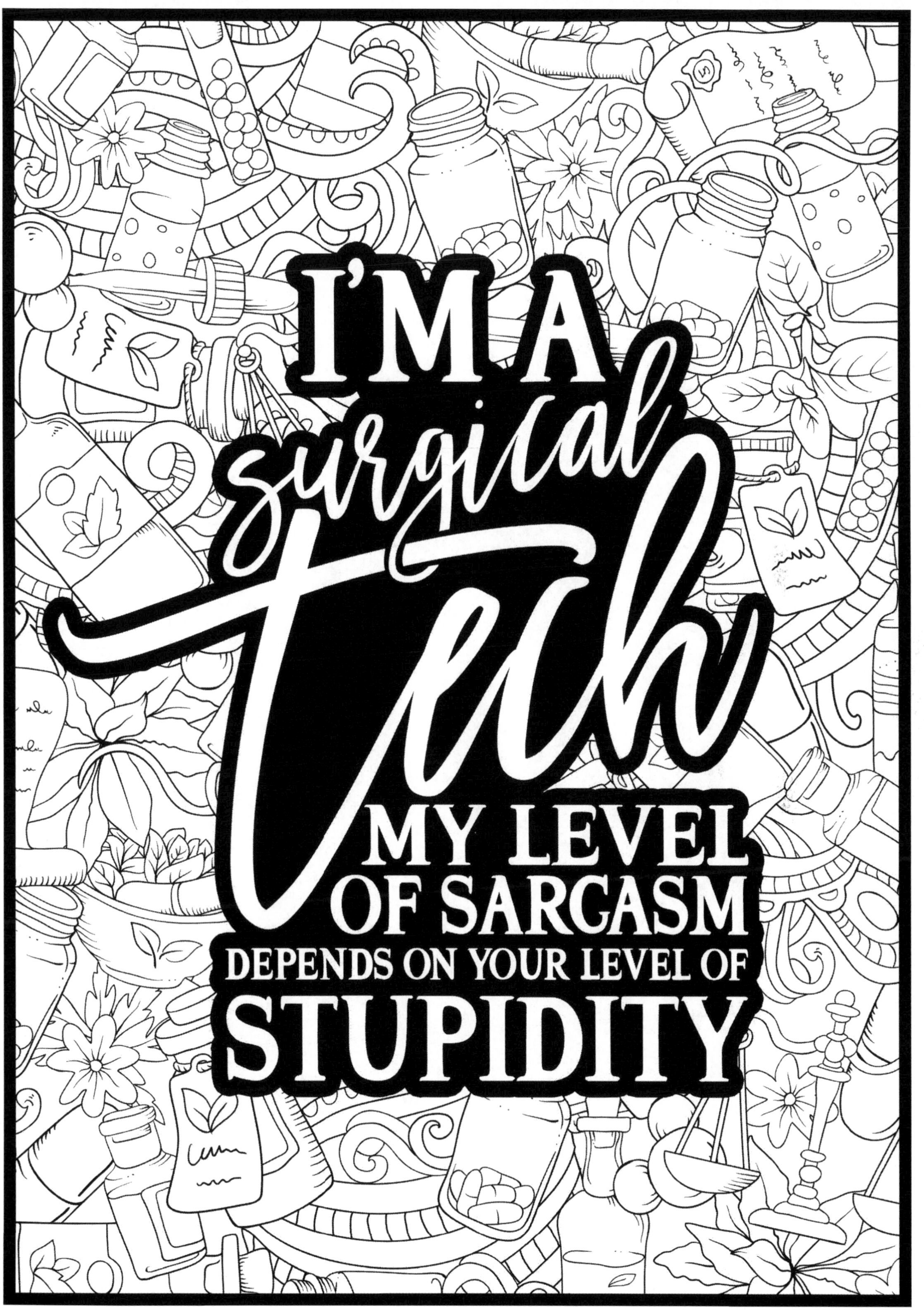
I'M A
surgical
tech
MY LEVEL
OF SARCASM
DEPENDS ON YOUR LEVEL OF
STUPIDITY

HOSPITAL
HOSPITAL

ALWAYS
BE NICE TO YOUR
SCRUB TECH
OR THEY'LL HAND YOU THE
SCALPEL
BY THE SHARP END!

When someone gets too close to my back table

scrub
HAIR
don't care

250ml

DOC, IF I DON'T
have it
YOU
DON'T
NEED IT

OMG! A SURGEON
ALMOST DIED IN FRONT OF ME TODAY!!!
But then I counted to 10 and put the scalpel down.
HE NEVER KNEW

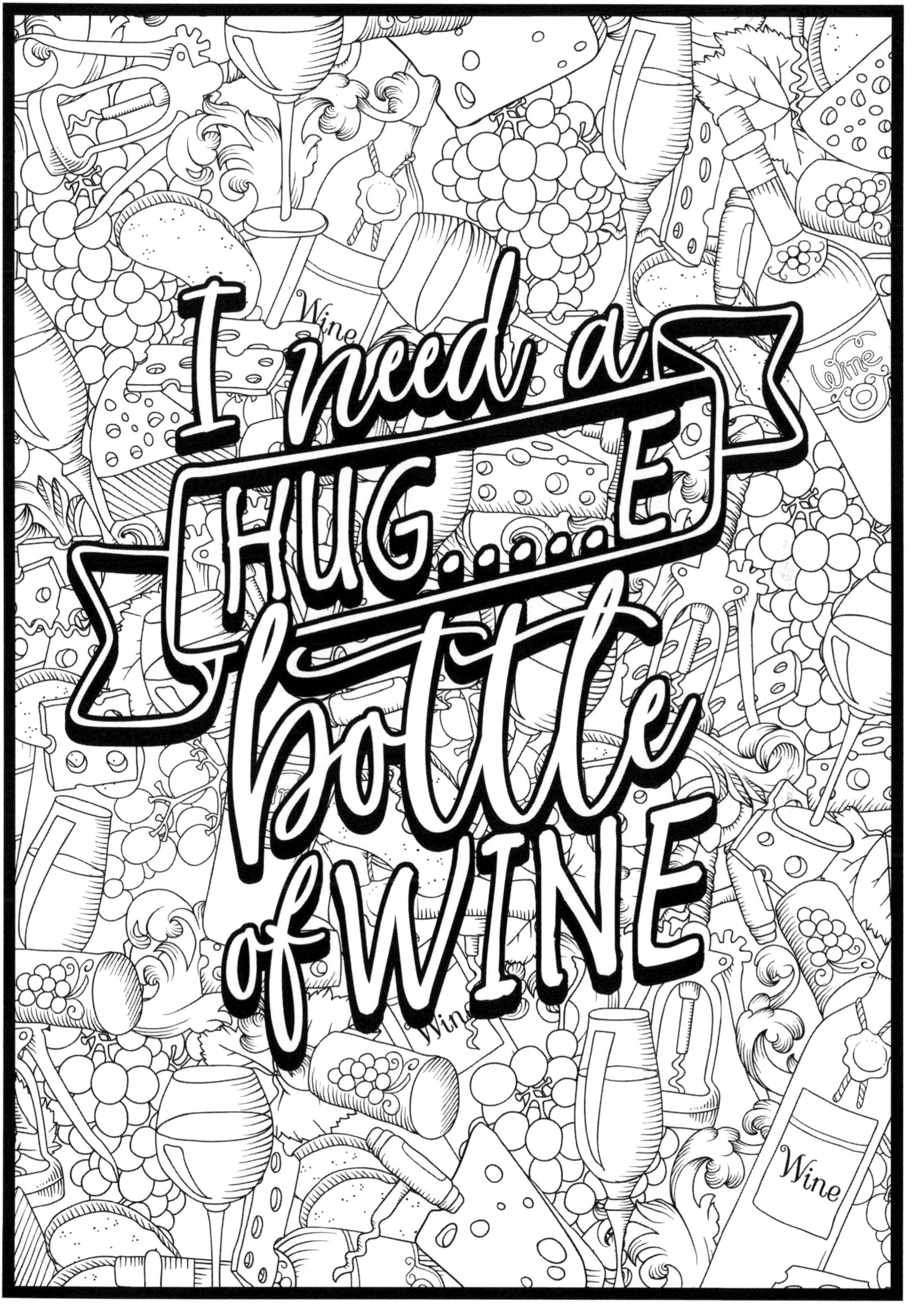
I need a
HUG.....E
bottle
of WINE
Wine
Wine

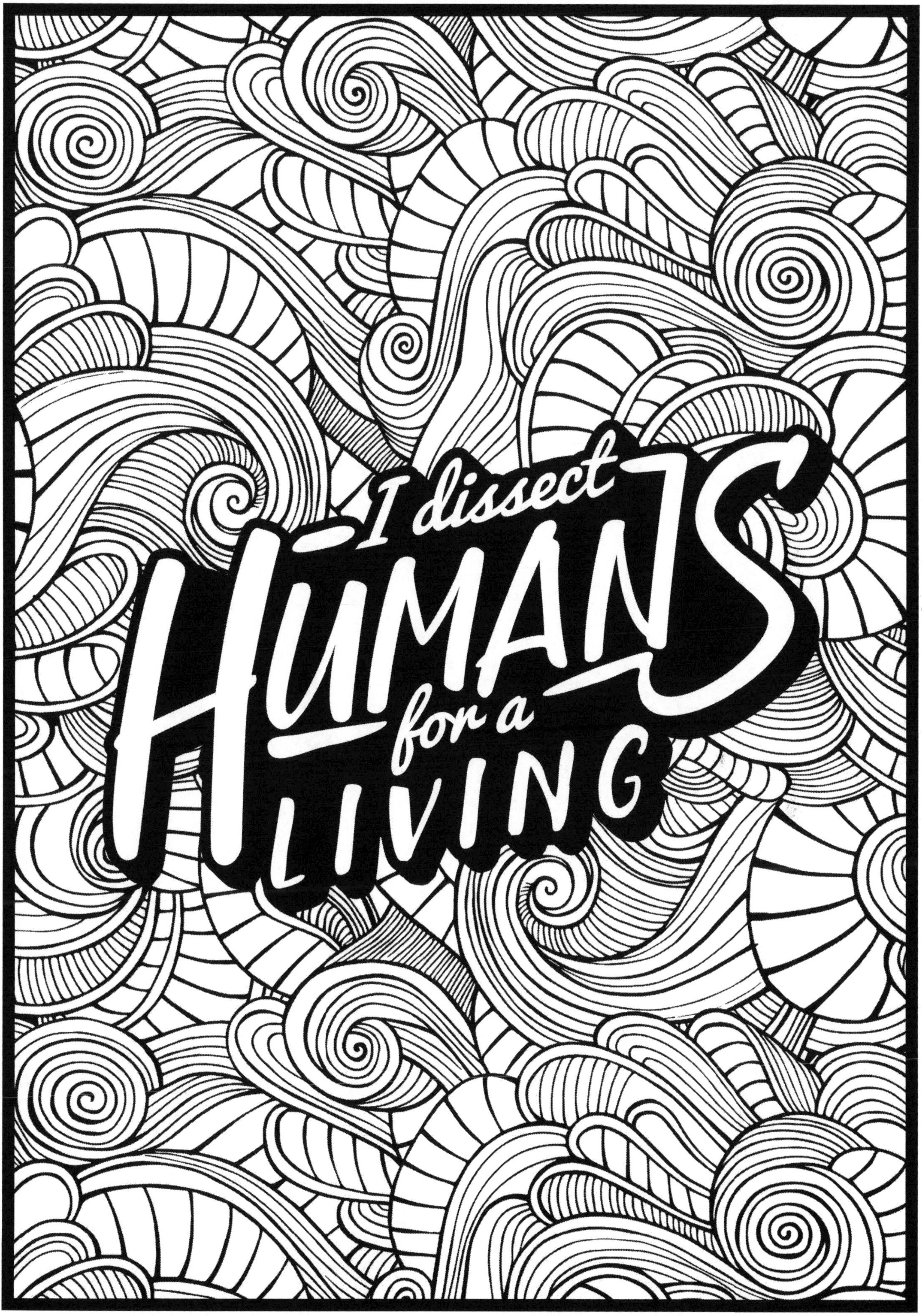
I dissect
HUMANS
for a
LIVING

WHEN THE SURGEON IS ARGUING
WITH ANESTHESIA
AND YOU'RE IN THE MIDDLE LIKE

HOSPITAL

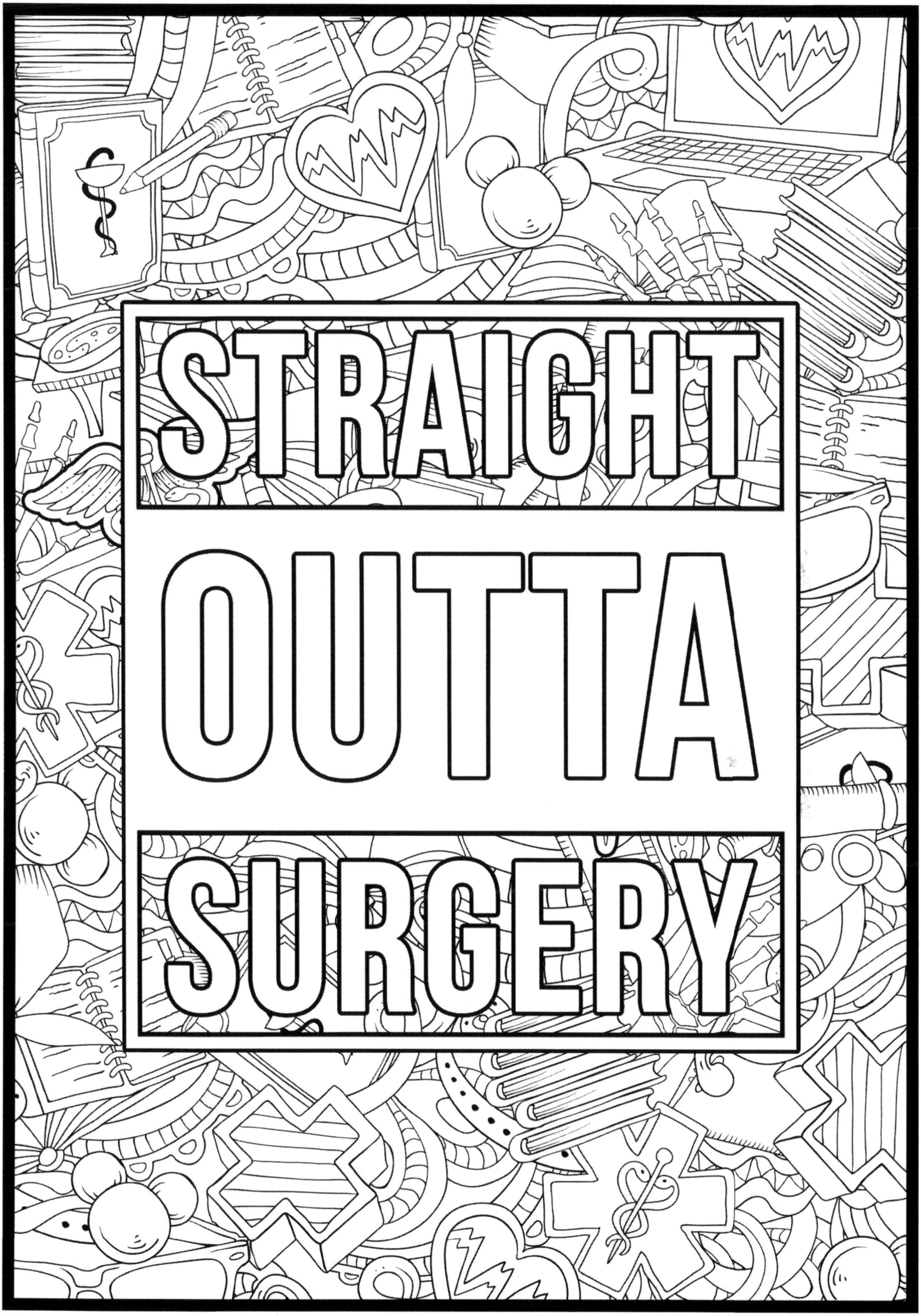
STRAIGHT
OUTTA
SURGERY

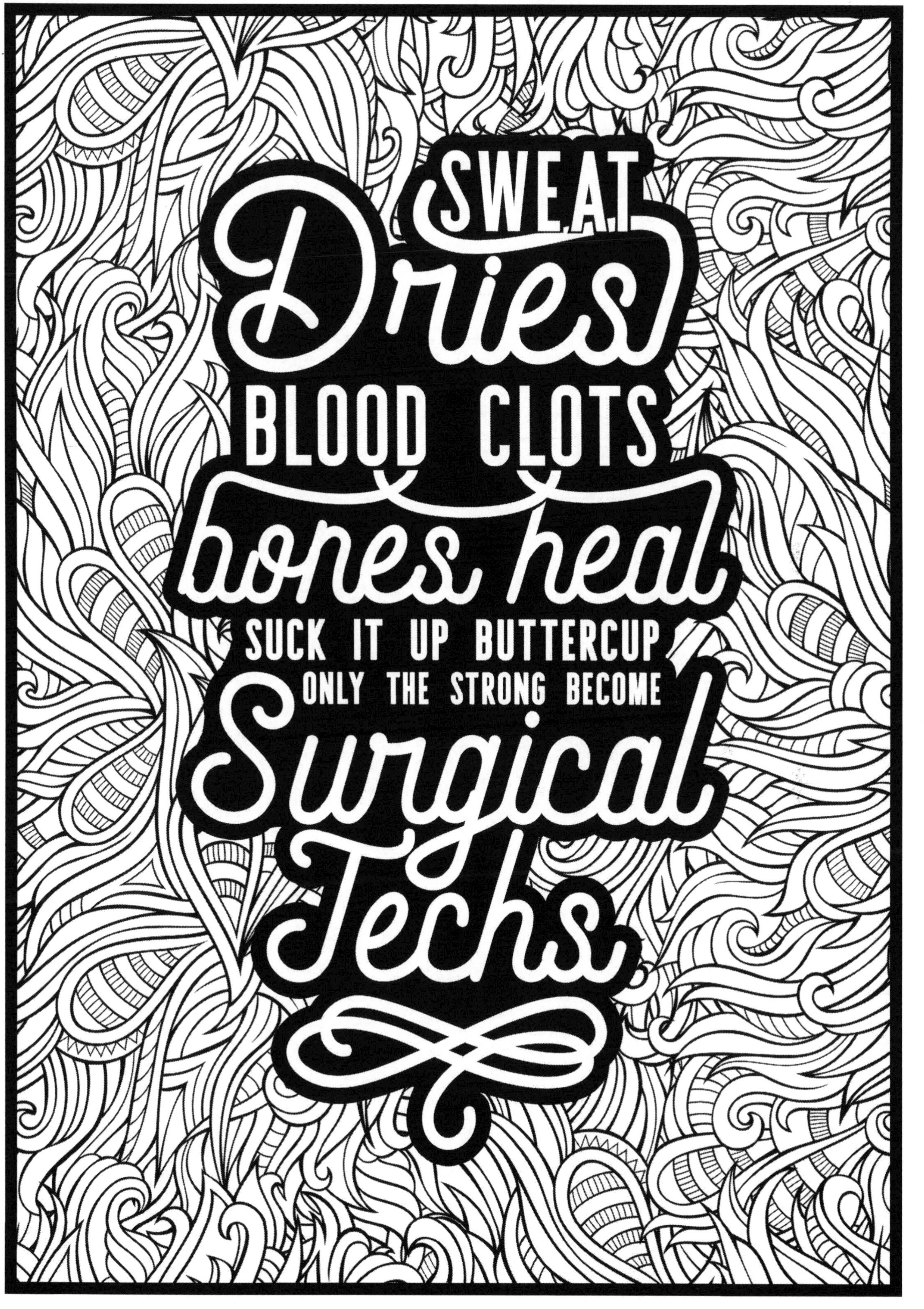
SWEAT
Dries
BLOOD CLOTS
bones heal
SUCK IT UP BUTTERCUP
ONLY THE STRONG BECOME
Surgical
Techs

BEHIND EVERY
GREAT SURGEON
THERE'S A TECH READING
THEIR FREAKING MIND

HOSPITAL

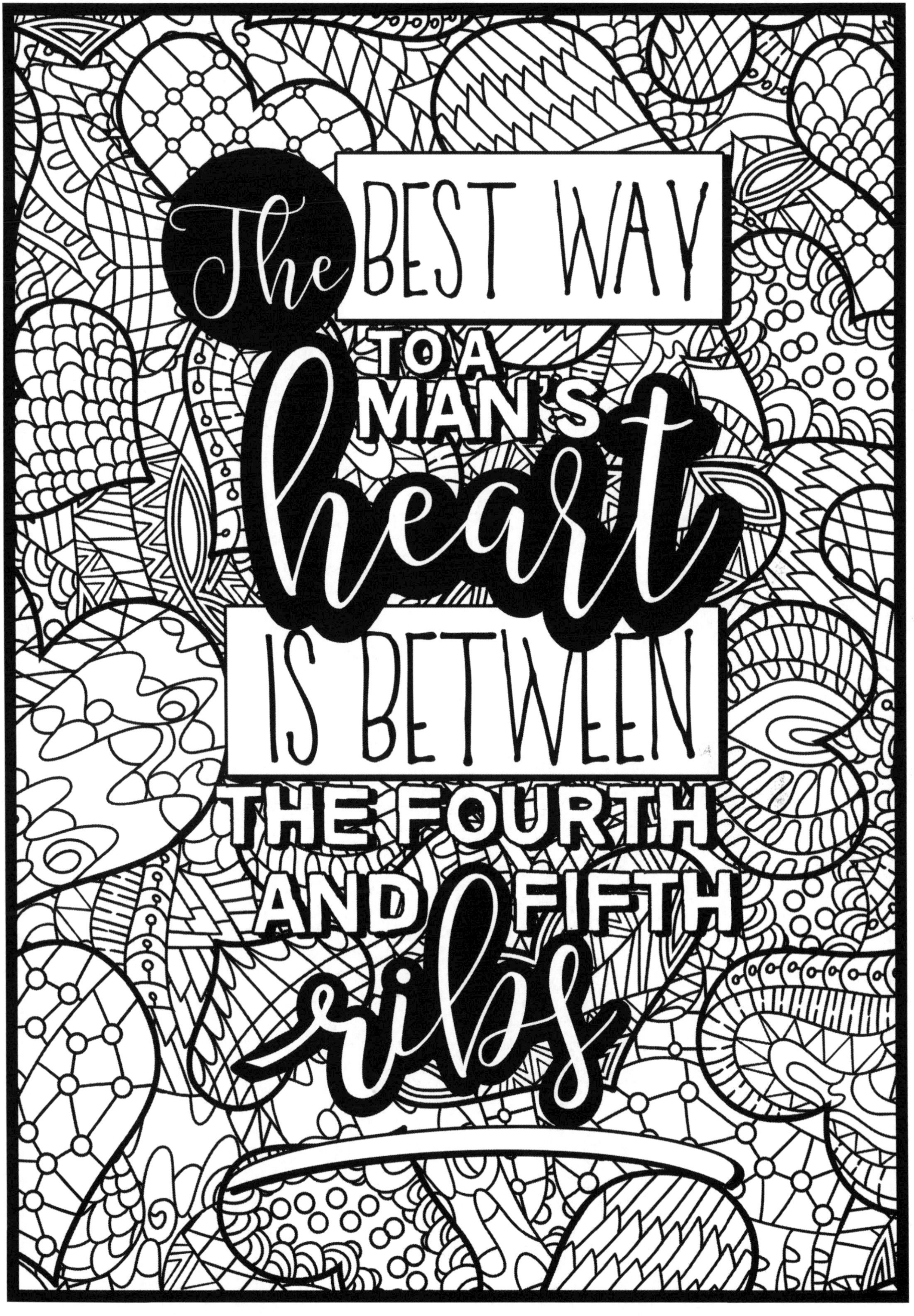
The BEST WAY
TO A MAN'S heart
IS BETWEEN
THE FOURTH AND FIFTH ribs

250ml

LIVIN' THE
SCRUB
LIFE

SAY
"I ALWAYS
DO IT THE
SAME WAY"
JUST ONE
MORE TIME...

36.6

Actually
MEDICINE
IS THE BEST
MEDICINE
36.6

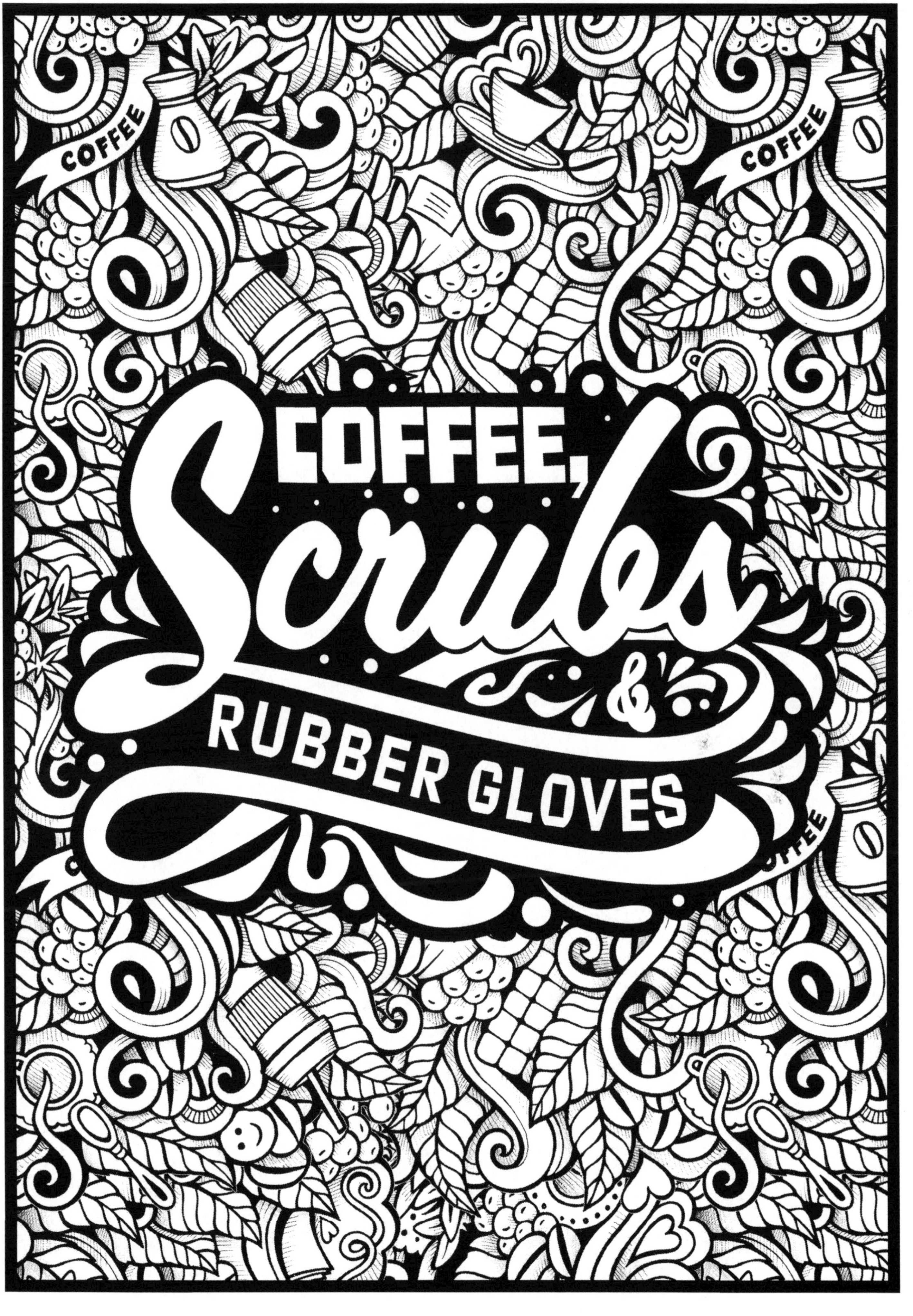
COFFEE,
Scrubs
&
RUBBER GLOVES
COFFEE
COFFEE
COFFEE

#thestruggleisreal
WHAT TO WEAR... WHAT TO WEAR...
#SCRUBLIFE

I LIKE PEOPLE.
ON THE TABLE.
OPEN.

BE NICE TO ME
I'M A
Surgical Tech
I KEEP
Doctors
FROM KILLING
-YOU-

I'M WAY
TOO
Sick
FOR WORK
BUT SHOULD
BE FINE FOR
Happy
Hour

250ml

JOHNNY HAS 12 CANDY BARS. HE EATS 10.

What does he have now?

oh snap!

I can't
BECAUSE
I'M ON
call

I'M CURRENTLY
EXPERIENCING
Life
at
the
SPEED
of 15 WTFs
Per Hour

WARNING
TO AVOID SERIOUS INJURY
DON'T TELL ME HOW
TO DO MY JOB

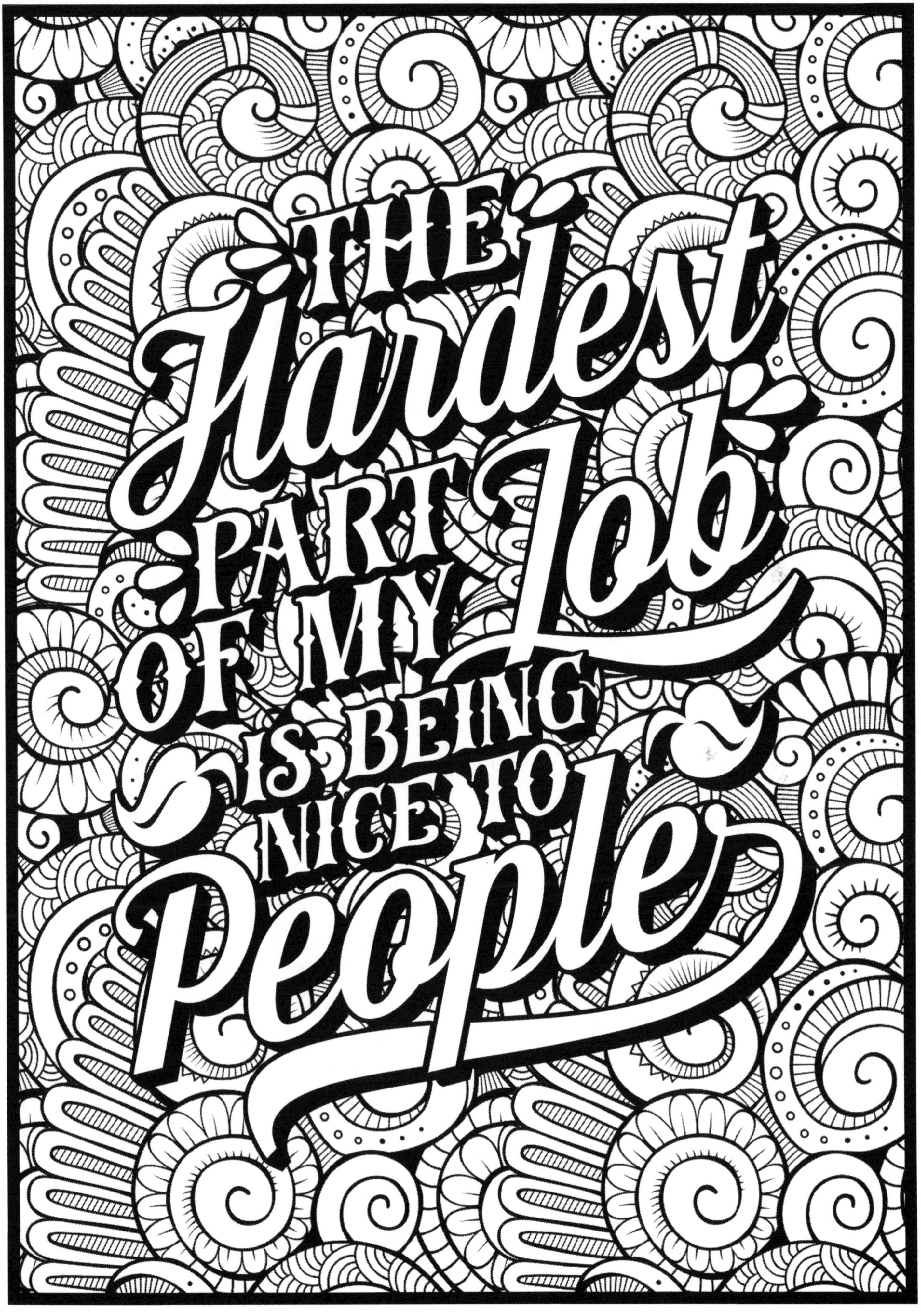
THE
Hardest
PART
OF MY
Job
IS BEING
NICE TO
People

HOSPITAL
HOSPITAL

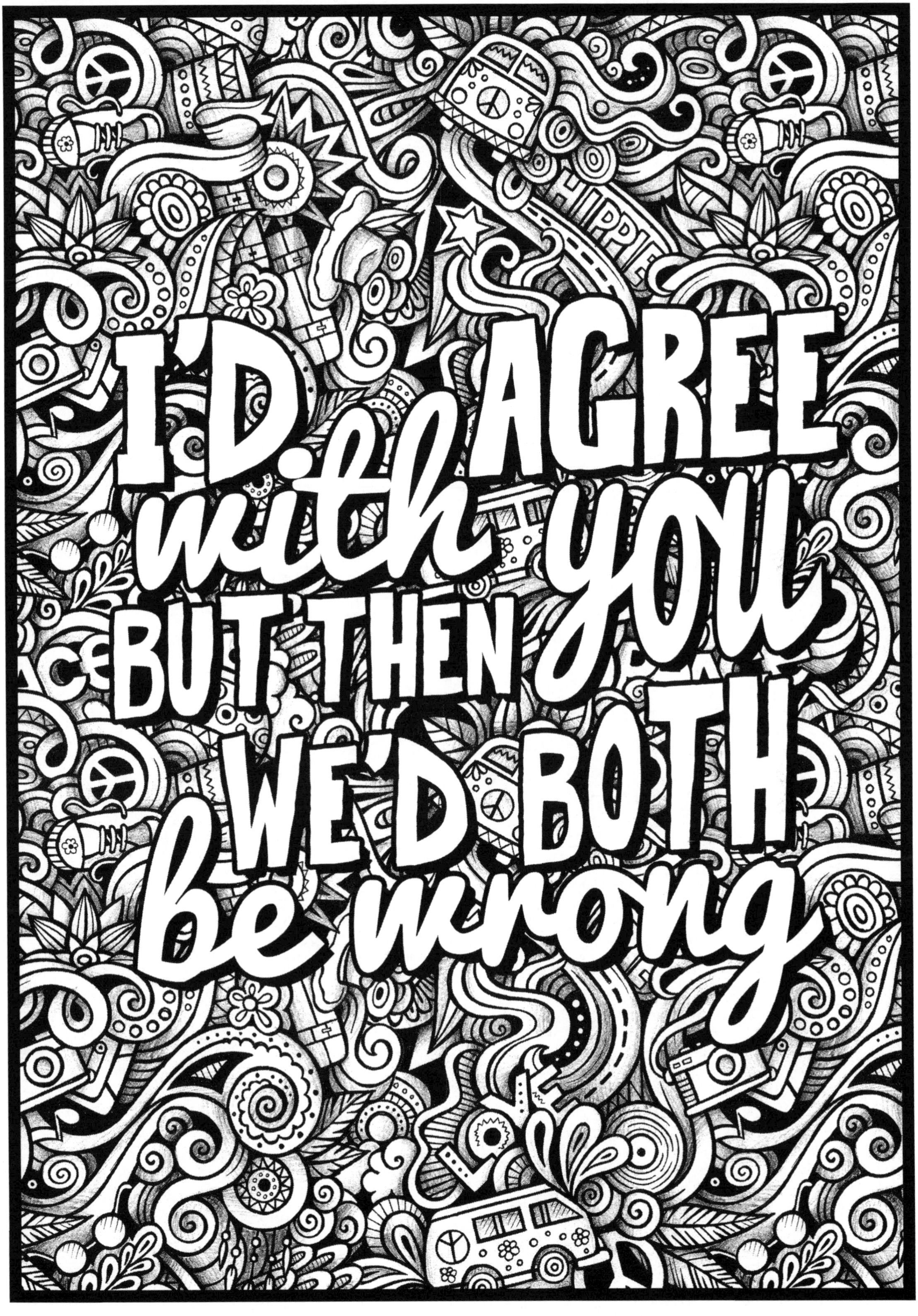
I'D AGREE
with you
BUT THEN
WE'D BOTH
be wrong

That moment
WHEN YOU HAVE TO
pee
REALLY BAD
BUT YOU CAN'T
GET THE DRAWSTRING
of your scrubs
UNTIED

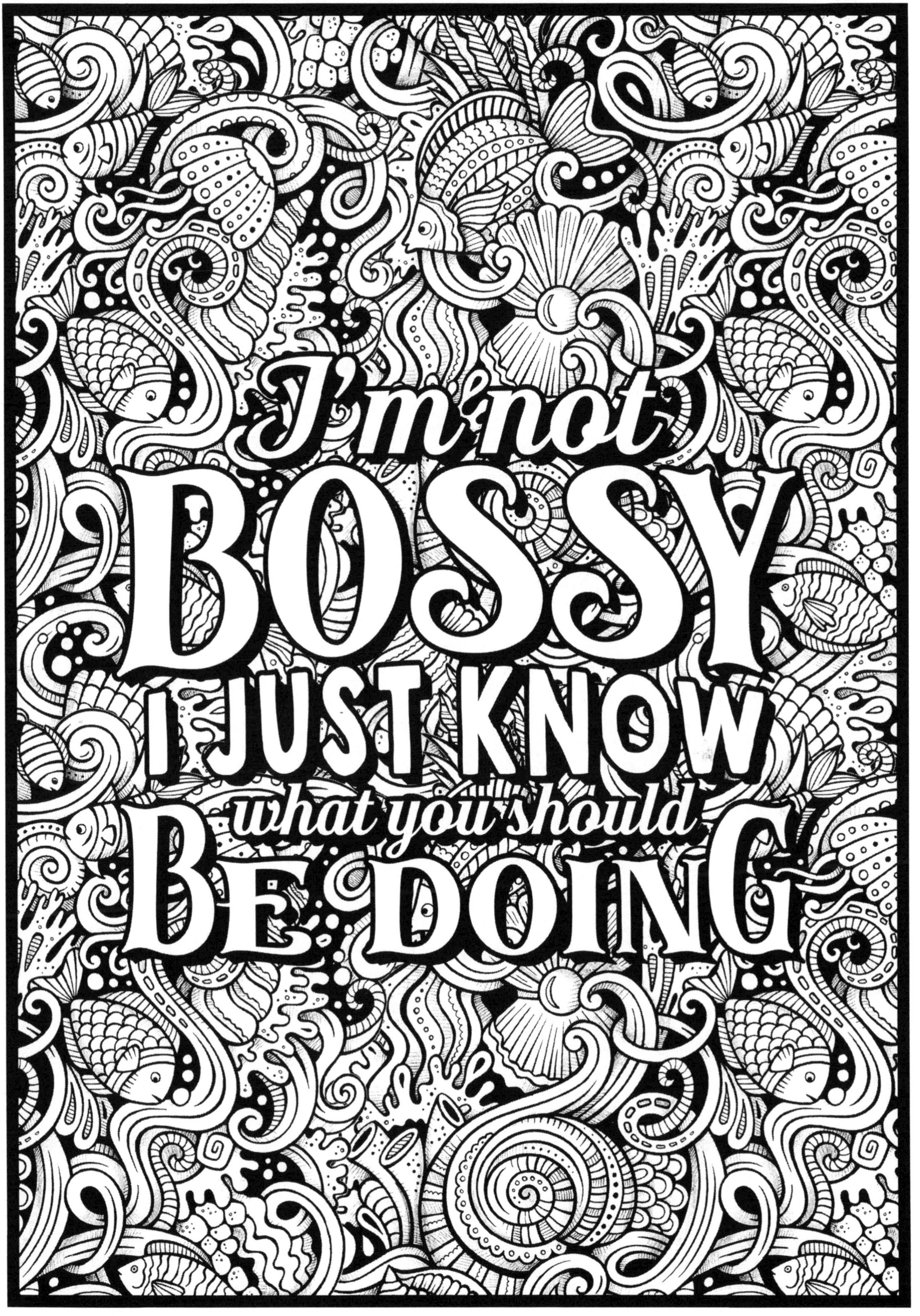
I'm not
BOSSY
I JUST KNOW
what you should
BE DOING

Studies say
SITTING
FOR LONG PERIODS
SHORTENS YOUR
LIFE.
Good news
SCRUB TECHS:
YOU'RE GOING TO LIVE
forever!

Nobody
PRESENTS
with a Mandibular
FRACTURE
WHO DIDN't
deserve
one

YOU don't have
to be CRAZY
to work here
WE'LL TRAIN YOU

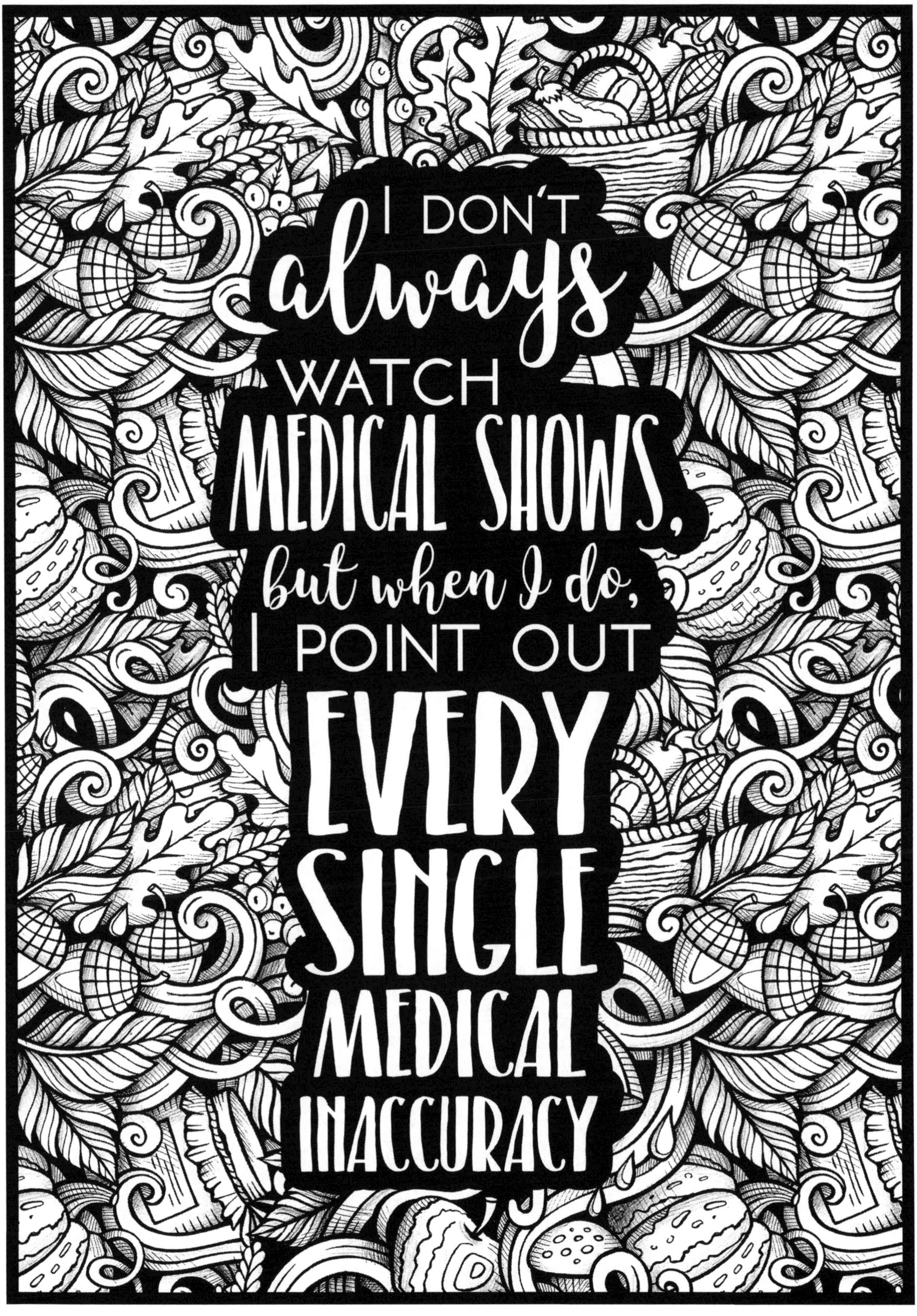
I DON'T
always
WATCH
MEDICAL SHOWS,
but when I do,
I POINT OUT
EVERY
SINGLE
MEDICAL
INACCURACY

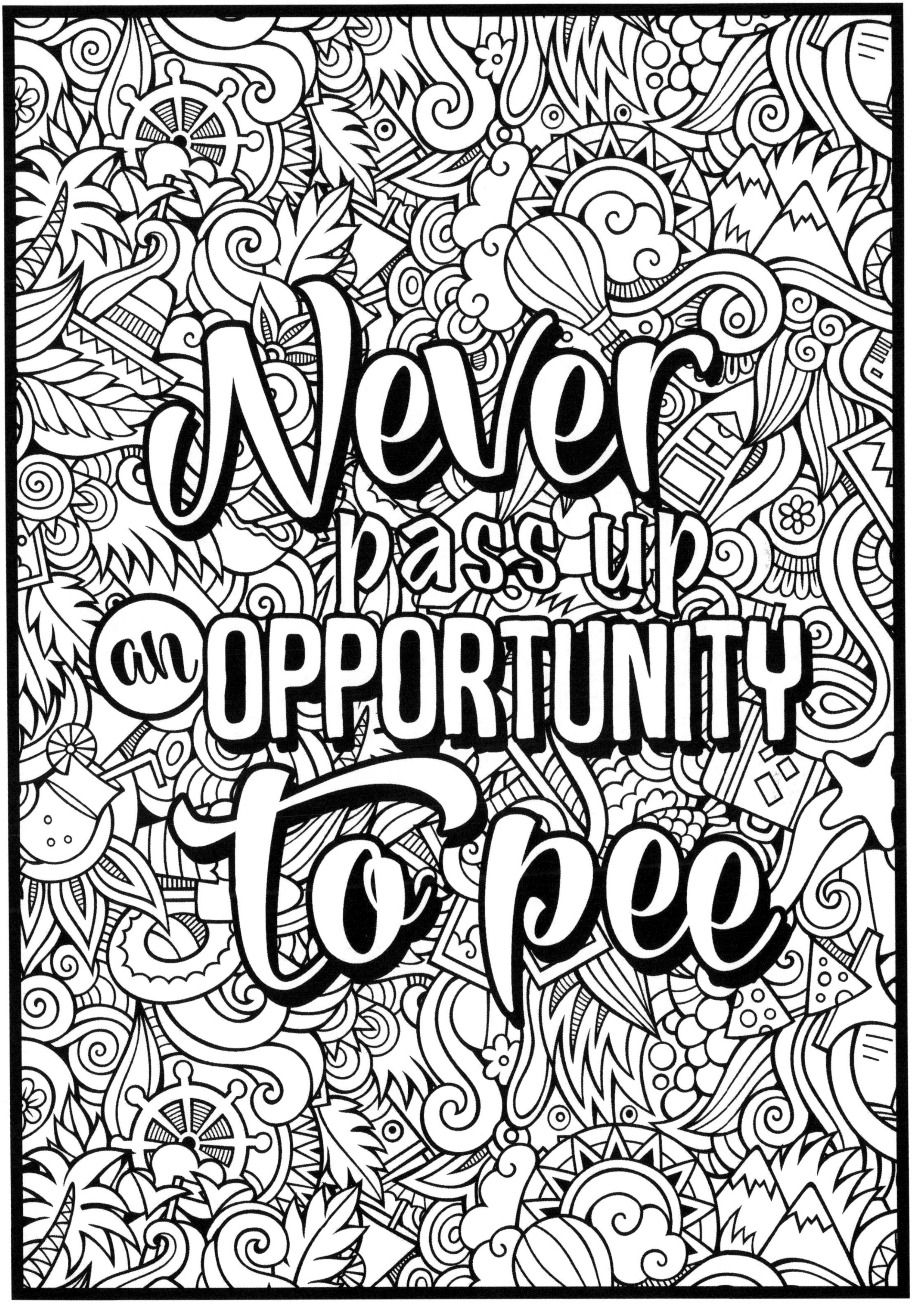
Never
pass up
an OPPORTUNITY
to pee

all bleeding
Stops
EVENTUALLY

HOSPITAL
HOSPITAL

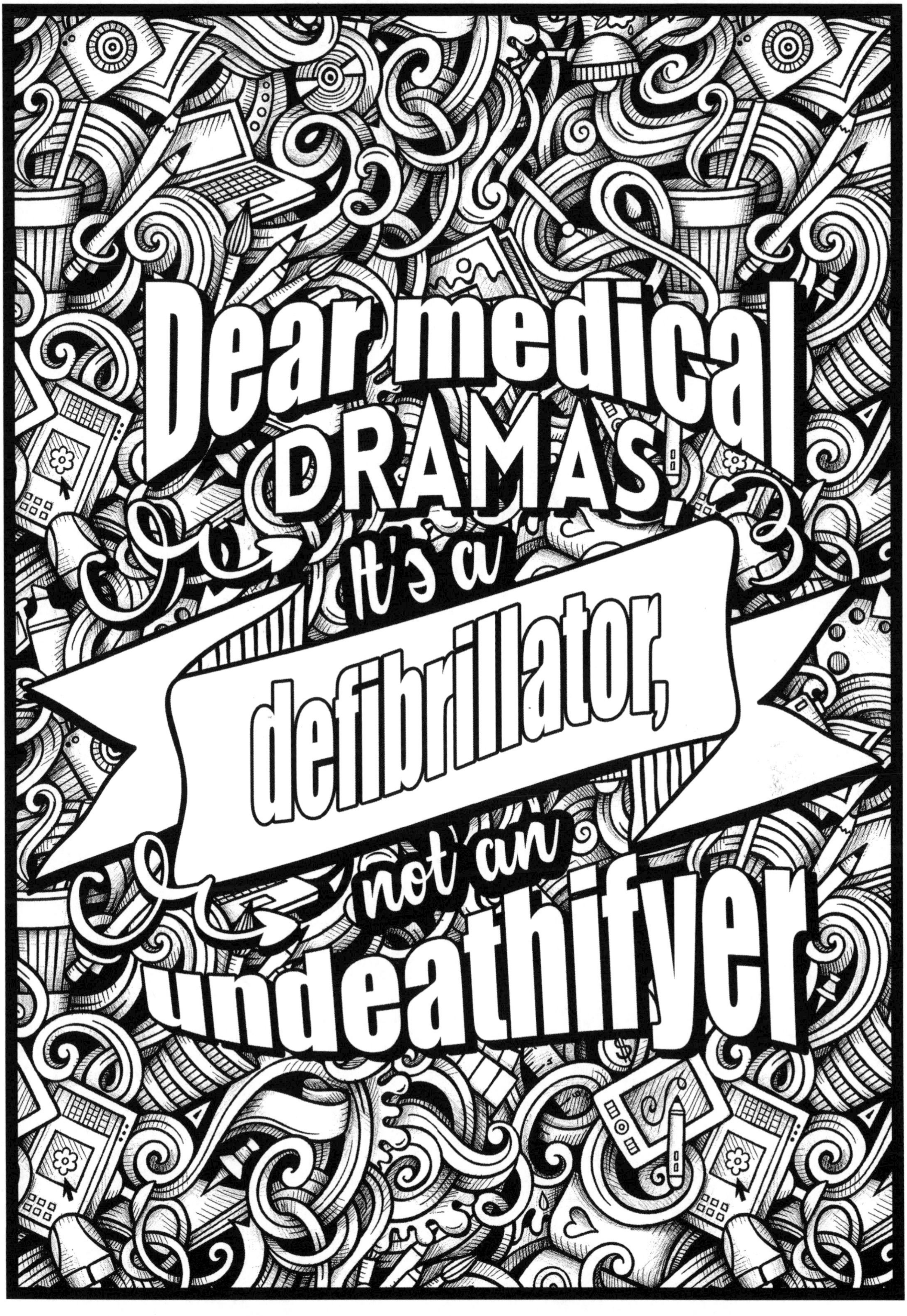
Dear medical
DRAMAS,
It's a
defibrillator,
not an
undeathifyer

FREE PDF DOWNLOAD OF THIS BOOK

www.pbleu.com/scrubtech

YOUR DOWNLOAD CODE: SCRUB373

@papeteriebleu

Papeterie Bleu

Want free goodies?
Email us at freebies@pbleu.com

@papeteriebleu

Papeterie Bleu

Shop our other books at
www.pbleu.com

Wholesale distribution through Ingram Content Group
www.ingramcontent.com/publishers/distribution/wholesale

For questions and customer service, email us at
support@pbleu.com

Made in the USA
Las Vegas, NV
20 February 2021

18200940R00059